CINNAMON BUN DREAMS

CINNAMON BUN DREAMS

A Comfort Food Coloring Book
by Squishable

THE COUNTRYMAN PRESS
A division of W. W. Norton & Company
Independent Publishers Since 1923

Printed in The United States of America

For information about permission to reproduce selections from
this book, write to Permissions, The Countryman Press,
500 Fifth Avenue, New York, NY 10110

For information about special discounts for bulk purchases, please contact
W. W. Norton Special Sales at specialsales@wwnorton.com or 800-233-4830

Manufacturing by RR Donnelley, Willard
Production manager: Devon Zahn

The Countryman Press
www.countrymanpress.com

A division of W. W. Norton & Company
500 Fifth Avenue, New York, NY 10110
www.wwnorton.com

978-1-682-68032-2 (pbk.)

10 9 8 7 6 5 4 3 2 1

Contents

Introduction

Comfort food! It's the secret snack, nibbled in front of the fridge! The smuggled slice of cake, munched under the covers by flashlight! The illicit cookies shared by friends, giggling as they keep watch for the hall monitor! The steaming bowl of noodle soup on a cold day! Comfort food is the culinary equivalent of a warm hug . . . for your mouth!

Cinnamon Bun Dreams is a collection of delicious designs from the art team at Squishable. We have spent a decade in intense experimentation over what exactly makes something adorable. Yes, cupcakes are cute, but what type of cupcake? What flavor of toaster tart? Smooth or crunchy peanut butter . . . which one is cuddlier? The world needs to know.

May you chew through these pages with an appetite. May they warm you, comfort you, and maybe make you a little hungry.

First we eat, then we do everything else.

— M. F. K. Fisher

Why, sometimes I've believed as many as
six impossible things before breakfast.

—Lewis Carroll

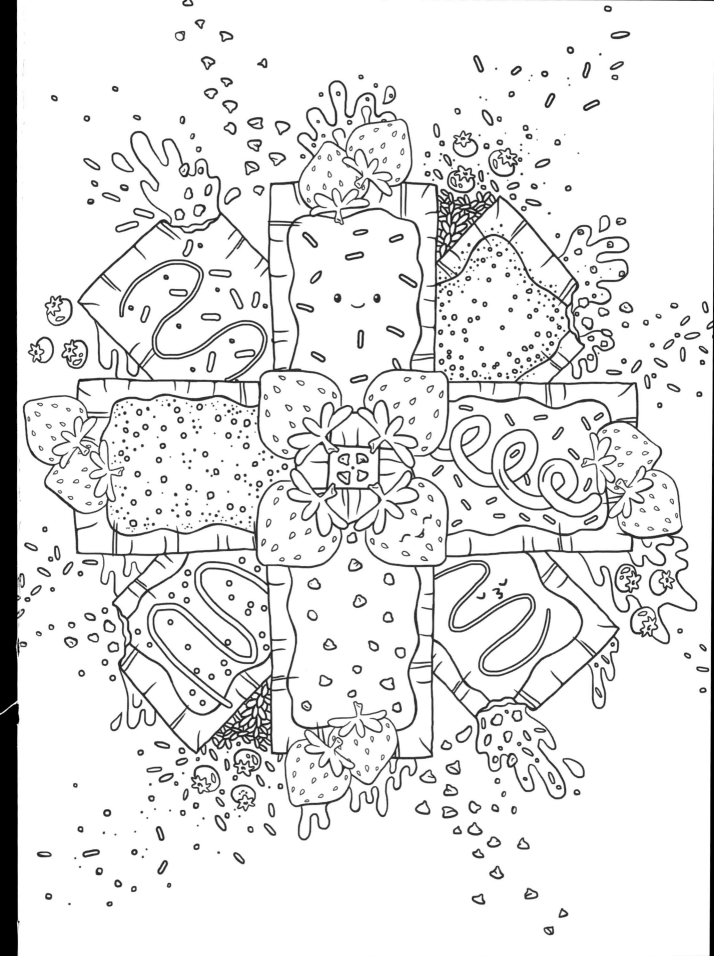

I like coffee because it gives me the
illusion that I might be awake.

—Lewis Black

Humor keeps us alive. Humor and food.
Don't forget food. You can go a week
without laughing.

—Joss Whedon

All happiness depends on
a leisurely breakfast.
—John Gunther

Part of the secret of success in life is to eat
what you like and let the food fight it out inside.

—Mark Twain

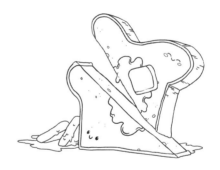

Bread and butter is my bread and butter.

—Unknown

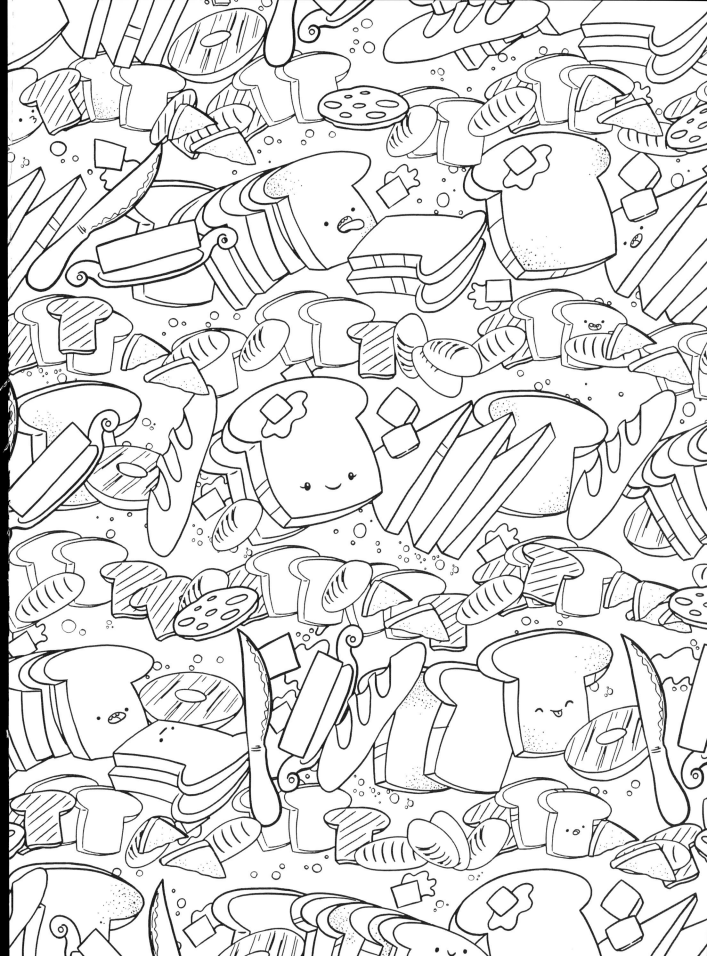

I'd rather take coffee than compliments just now.

—Louisa May Alcott

Forbidden fruit is the sweetest.

—Proverb

Time is an illusion. Lunchtime, doubly so.

—Douglas Adams

You better cut the pizza in four pieces
because I'm not hungry enough to eat six.

—Yogi Berra

I will gladly pay you Tuesday for a hamburger today.

—J. Wellington "Wimpy"

The Kraken stirs. And ten billion sushi
dinners cry out for vengeance.

—Sir Terry Pratchett

Woe to the cook whose sauce has no sting.

—Geoffrey Chaucer

There is no love sincerer than the love of food.
—George Bernard Shaw

An ounce of sauce covers a multitude of sins.

—Anthony Bourdain

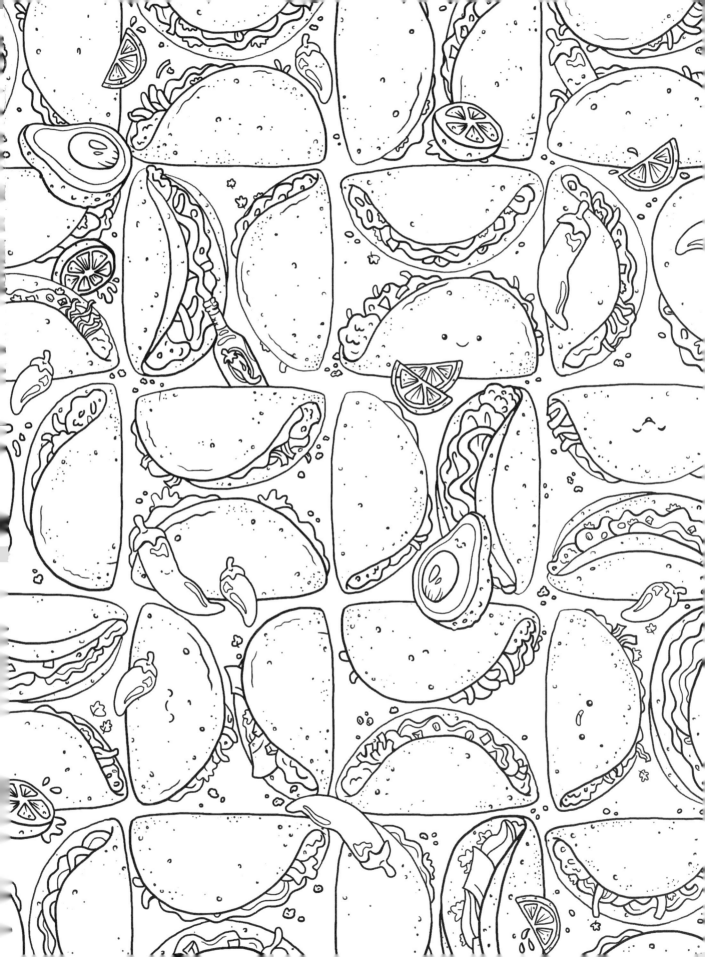

Life is uncertain. Eat dessert first.

—Ernestine Ulmer

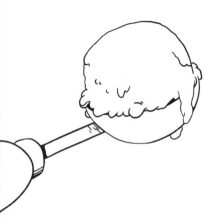

When I'm no longer rapping, I want to open up an
ice cream parlor and call myself Scoop Dogg.

—Snoop Dogg

Chocolate remedies adversity.

—Jareb Teague

A balanced diet is a cookie in each hand.

—Barbara Johnson

My advice to you is not to inquire why or whither,
but just enjoy your ice cream while it's on your plate.

—Thornton Wilder

Life is so much better with whipped cream on top.

—Unknown

A party without cake is just a meeting.

—Julia Child

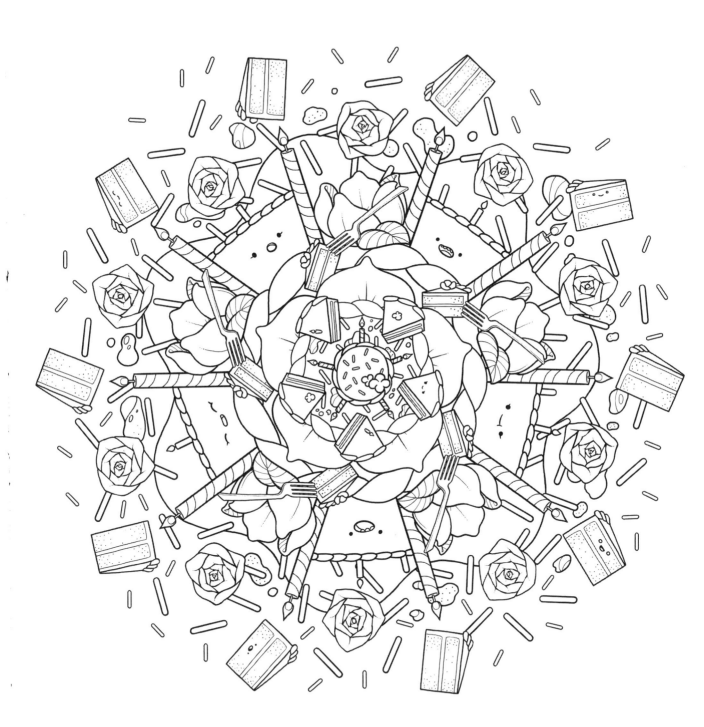

Almost every person has something
secret he likes to eat.

—M. F. K. Fisher

Life's no piece of cake, mind you,
but the recipe's my own to fool with.

—Haruki Murakami

Promises and pie-crust are made to be broken.

—Jonathan Swift

If you wish to make an apple pie from scratch,
you must first invent the universe.

—Carl Sagan

Ice-cream is exquisite. What a pity it isn't illegal.

—Voltaire

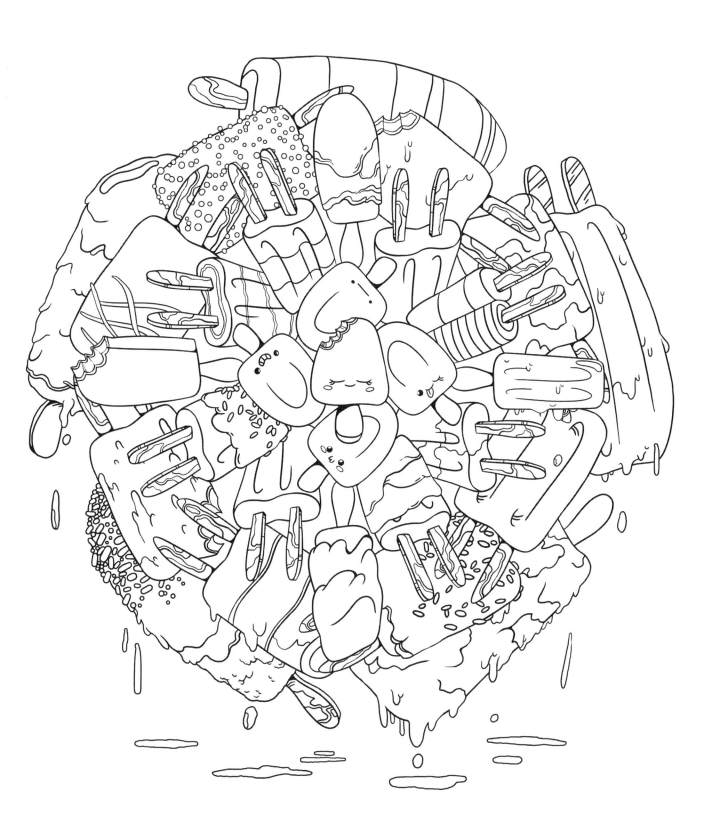

People who love to eat are always the best people.

—Julia Child

Don't wreck a sublime chocolate
experience by feeling guilty.

—Lora Brody

Stress cannot exist in the presence of a pie.
—David Mamet

The Artists

Zoe Fraade-Blanar, Editor

Sam Cooper

Pat Hughes

Elena Ferri

Jenna Howard

Melissa Gonnella

Katie Diamond

Rachel Briggs

Maybel Kwok

Ann Faris

Kerstin Ruthberg

Nathaniel Manns

Lindsay Barckholtz

Marie Dirvin

Acknowledgments

Cinnamon Bun Dreams: A Comfort Food Coloring Book exists because the following people were both very kind and very enthusiastic: Ann Treistman, Anne Somlyo, Brendan Curry, Joe Lops, and Anna Reich at W. W. Norton, and Zoë Pagnamenta and Alison Lewis at the Zoë Pagnamenta Agency.

Thank you to the entire Squishable team, past and present: Elizabeth Barnes, Sam Cooper, Brian Cross, Charles Donefer, Elena Ferri, Zoe Fraade-Blanar, Aaron M. Glazer, Melissa Gonnella, Anastasia Holl, Eric Holland, Jenna Howard, Pat Hughes, Russell Pinke, Beth Roberts, Christopher Santulli, Rishika Singh, Debbie Stair, Scott Watson, and Kendra Wells.

This book is also thanks to the artists who originally created these characters. Some come from the Squishable staff, but many are thanks to the thousands of designers who gave their time and creativity to submit their ideas to Project Open Squish, the Squishable crowdsourcing platform. You create some cute stuff, people.

And thank you to the entire Squishable Nation, a million strong and still growing. When fans first asked us to do a coloring book, we said "yeah!," and then procrastinated about it for a decade. It is only with their constant support, encouragement, and occasional gifts of chocolate that this lovely book was made. To every fan: thank you truly, deeply, from the very bottom of our squishy, squishy hearts.